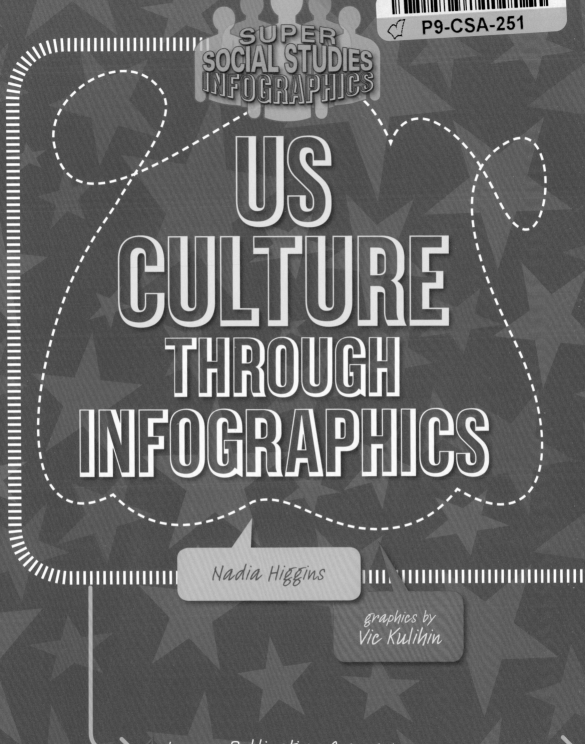

SUPER
SOCIAL STUDIES
INFOGRAPHICS

P9-CSA-251

US CULTURE THROUGH INFOGRAPHICS

Nadia Higgins

graphics by
Vic Kulihin

Lerner Publications Company
Minneapolis

Lerner Publications Company
A division of Lerner Publishing Group, Inc.
241 First Avenue North
Minneapolis, MN USA 55401

For reading levels and more information, look up this title at
www.lernerbooks.com.

Main text set in Univers LT Std 12/15.
Typeface provided by Adobe Systems.

Library of Congress Cataloging-in-Publication Data

Higgins, Nadia.
    US culture through infographics / by Nadia Higgins ; illustrated by Vic
Kulihin.
        pages   cm. — (Super social studies infographics)
    Includes index.
    ISBN 978–1–4677–3464–6 (lib. bdg. : alk. paper)
    ISBN 978–1–4677–4746–2 (eBook)
    1. United States—Social life and customs—Juvenile literature. 2. Popular
culture—United States—Juvenile literature. 3. Information visualization—
Juvenile literature. I. Kulihin, Vic, illustrator. II. Title.
E169.Z83H54 2015
306.0973—dc23   2013044338

Manufactured in the United States of America
1 – PC – 7/15/14

CONTENTS

Introduction: Study America • 4

ALL-AMERICAN PIES • 6

A TOUR OF CULTURES • 8

HOW WE RELAX • 10

AMERICAN ART FORMS • 12

PLAY BALL! • 14

WHAT TO READ? • 16

LET'S CELEBRATE! • 18

Index • 32
Further Information • 31
Glossary • 30

BE A STAR CITIZEN • 28

PROTECT MY RIGHTS! • 26

PATRIOTIC DOS AND DON'TS • 24

KNOW YOUR SYMBOLS • 22

AMERICAN LANDMARKS • 20

STUDY AMERICA

Do you have a future as an expert in American culture? To find out, take this test!

1. Do you like to talk about movies as much as you like to watch them?

2. Have you ever memorized the words to a Broadway song?

3. Do you love reading great American authors, from Shel Silverstein to Laura Ingalls Wilder?

4. Are you fascinated by the range of traditions among your friends' families?

Did you answer yes to any of those questions?

CONGRATULATIONS!

You just might have what it takes to be an American studies scholar. American studies is a broad field that looks at US culture from dozens of angles. Experts in the field study American literature, arts, and symbols—to name a few. They look at American attitudes, pastimes, and habits. They also study how people of all ethnic backgrounds come together to create our unique American culture.

That's a lot to keep straight! Luckily, infographics can help. Charts, graphs, and other infographics are a visual way to organize information about US culture. Are you ready to join in the fun? Let's get started!

ALL-AMERICAN PIES

Americans come from a huge variety of backgrounds—different ethnic groups, family sizes, incomes, religions, and more. Let's take a look at how diverse Americans can be. *(Note that total percentages may not equal 100, due to rounding.)*

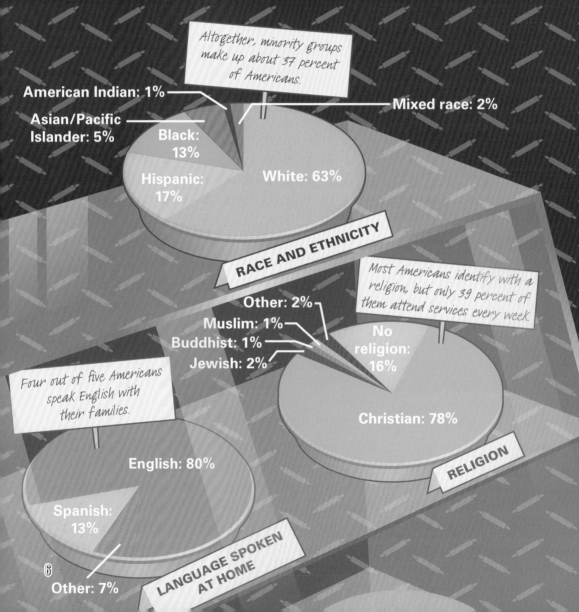

Altogether, minority groups make up about 37 percent of Americans.

American Indian: 1%

Asian/Pacific Islander: 5%

Mixed race: 2%

Black: 13%

Hispanic: 17%

White: 63%

RACE AND ETHNICITY

Most Americans identify with a religion, but only 39 percent of them attend services every week.

Other: 2%

Muslim: 1%

Buddhist: 1%

Jewish: 2%

No religion: 16%

Christian: 78%

RELIGION

Four out of five Americans speak English with their families.

English: 80%

Spanish: 13%

Other: 7%

LANGUAGE SPOKEN AT HOME

The percentage of Americans who live out in the country is at an all-time low.

Rural (small towns and farms): 16%

Urban (cities): 33%

Suburbs (towns just outside of cities): 51%

URBAN, RURAL, SUBURBAN

Single mom and kids: 12.1%

There's no single type of family in the United States.

What kind of pet?
Dogs: 69%
Cats: 51%
Fish: 11%
Birds: 7%
Other: 8%

Unmarried parents and kids: 2.2%

Single dad and kids: 2.3%

Grandparents raising kids: 1.5%

Married couple with kids: 28.6%

Three out of five Americans own pets.

Parents and adult children living together: 9.5%

Married couple without children at home*: 42.8%

Pets: 62%

No pets: 38%

FAMILY

*Includes couples with no children as well as those with adult children living separately.

PET OWNERS

UNIQUELY AMERICAN

As an American, you perform customs you probably don't even think about. Here are some American customs that may seem out of place in other parts of the world:

wearing shorts

putting your feet on a chair

eating while walking down the street

tipping servers

7

A TOUR OF CULTURES

You don't need to leave the country to experience a variety of rich cultures. Chances are, people in your community come from several different ethnic backgrounds. Take a tour of some of the diverse communities here in the United States.

SOMALI

Minneapolis, Minnesota

Fact: The largest community of Somalis outside of Africa is found here.

See and do: Have a cup of sweet tea at the Karmel Square Somali Mall.

CHINESE

San Francisco's Chinatown, California

Fact: This is the nation's largest community of Chinese Americans.

See and do: Gape at the acrobats, stilt walkers, and floats in the Chinese New Year Parade held each spring.

KOREAN

Koreatown, Los Angeles, California

Fact: The country's largest community of Korean Americans is in this part of California.

See and do: Buy a jar of kimchi, a traditional dish made of fermented cabbage and spices.

HISPANIC

New Mexico

Fact: One out of two New Mexicans is Hispanic.

See and do: Visit the National Hispanic Cultural Center in Albuquerque to see what's new in the world of Hispanic art.

GERMAN

Milwaukee, Wisconsin

Fact: German settlers built this city in the mid-1800s.

See and do: In July, stop by the German Fest and check out famous German cars.

ARAB

Dearborn, Michigan

Fact: One-third of the city is Arab American.

See and do: Visit the only museum in America devoted to the Arab American experience.

IRISH

Boston, Massachusetts

Fact: Boston boasts the highest concentration of Irish Americans of any city.

See and do: Watch Irish step dancers during Boston's huge St. Patrick's Day celebration.

ITALIAN

Little Italy, Providence, Rhode Island

Fact: The neighborhood is a hub for Italian restaurants and bakeries.

See and do: On March 19, celebrate the Feast of St. Joseph with some sugary *zeppole*—pastries of deep-fried dough.

AMERICAN INDIAN

Navajo Nation

Fact: The Navajo have the largest reservation in the United States

See and do: Cheer on the rodeo stars at the annual Navajo Nation Fair.

AFRICAN AMERICAN

Harlem, New York City

Fact: A center of black culture has thrived here since the 1910s.

See and do: Take in a world-class show by African American artists at the Apollo Theater.

HOW WE RELAX

The average American spends 9 hours, 12 minutes, and 36 seconds working and getting to and from work every day. Americans are known for putting in long hours, but they play hard too. Free time activities tend to vary based on gender and age.

WEEKENDS

On a typical weekend day, men relax for 1 hour and 23 minutes more than women. Women watch less TV, but men get more exercise.

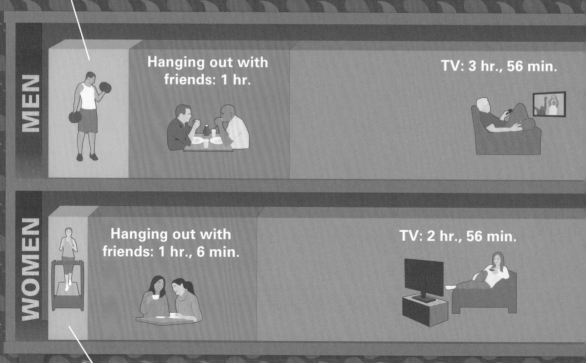

MEN

Sports and exercise: 32 min.

Hanging out with friends: 1 hr.

TV: 3 hr., 56 min.

WOMEN

Hanging out with friends: 1 hr., 6 min.

TV: 2 hr., 56 min.

Sports and exercise: 13 min.

TV BY THE NUMBERS

The United States has more TVs than people—and that's not even counting phones and other devices. Watching TV and videos—either online or on the tube—is definitely America's No. 1 pastime.

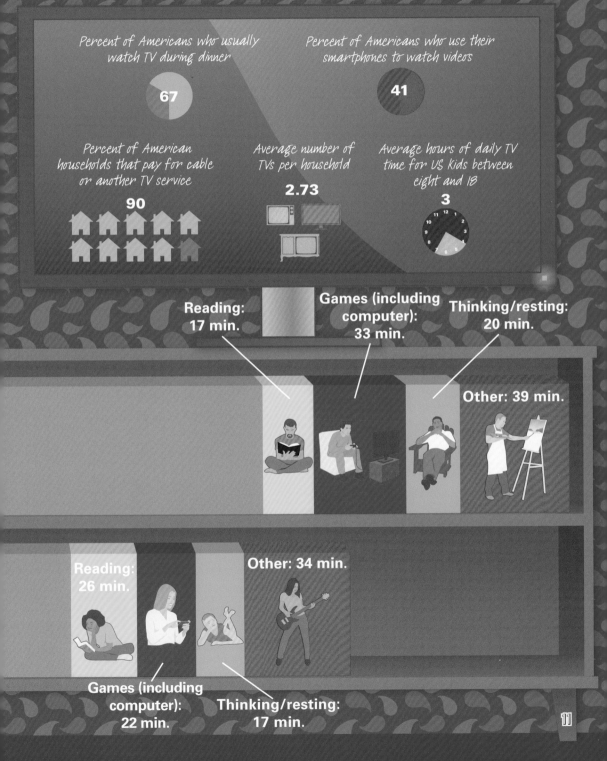

Percent of Americans who usually watch TV during dinner

67

Percent of Americans who use their smartphones to watch videos

41

Percent of American households that pay for cable or another TV service

90

Average number of TVs per household

2.73

Average hours of daily TV time for US kids between eight and 18

3

Reading: 17 min.

Games (including computer): 33 min.

Thinking/resting: 20 min.

Other: 39 min.

Reading: 26 min.

Other: 34 min.

Games (including computer): 22 min.

Thinking/resting: 17 min.

AMERICAN ART FORMS

The United States has fostered a lot of creativity over the centuries! About 100 years ago, four art forms were born right here on US soil. Check out how these American art forms have grown over the years and remained vital parts of American culture.

Jazz

Jazz is a form of music that grew out of black slave songs and African beats. It's known for unexpected rhythms and improvisation (making up music on the fly).

early 1900s: Jazz begins in New Orleans, Louisiana.

1927: *Show Boat* breaks new ground with its complex story and attention to racial issues

Musical Theater

Musical theater tells stories through both talking and singing. Broadway shows feature catchy songs, often with lots of dancing and plenty of laughs.

late 1800s: Musical theater begins in New York City.

LATE 1800s — 1900 — 1910 — 1920 — 1930

Movies

Movies tell stories through filmed images. They feature interesting camera angles, close-ups, and special effects. Music heightens the action.

1910s: Full-length, silent movies begin in Hollywood.

late 1920s: "Talking pictures"—movies with sound—mark a turning point in film.

Modern Dance

Modern dance features interesting movements, simple costumes, and bare feet. It began in opposition to ballet and was pioneered by women. That meant a lot in the early 1900s, when female artists usually took a backseat to men.

Early 1900s: American dancer Isadora Duncan introduces modern dance.

1930s: Martha Graham's modern dance features sharp, angular movements and long, draped costumes.

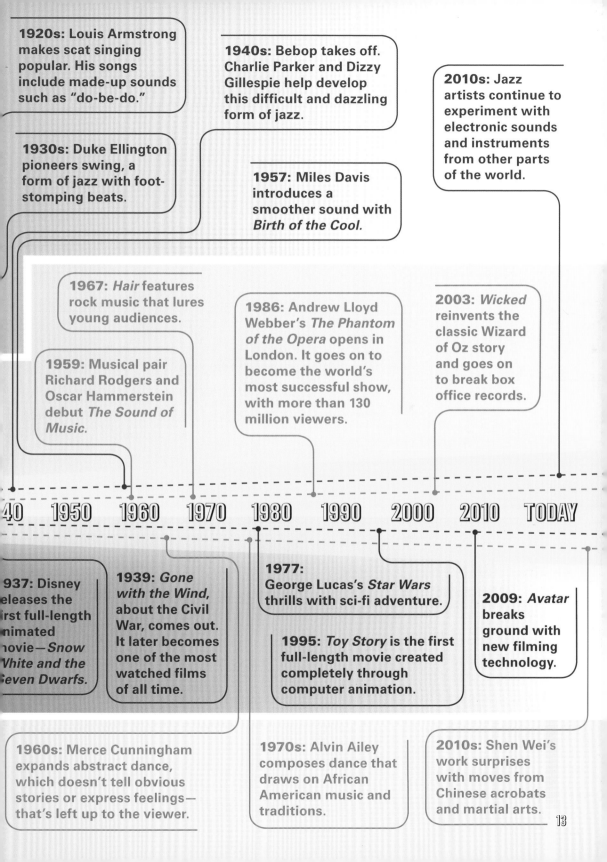

1920s: Louis Armstrong makes scat singing popular. His songs include made-up sounds such as "do-be-do."

1940s: Bebop takes off. Charlie Parker and Dizzy Gillespie help develop this difficult and dazzling form of jazz.

2010s: Jazz artists continue to experiment with electronic sounds and instruments from other parts of the world.

1930s: Duke Ellington pioneers swing, a form of jazz with foot-stomping beats.

1957: Miles Davis introduces a smoother sound with *Birth of the Cool.*

1967: *Hair* features rock music that lures young audiences.

1986: Andrew Lloyd Webber's *The Phantom of the Opera* opens in London. It goes on to become the world's most successful show, with more than 130 million viewers.

2003: *Wicked* reinvents the classic Wizard of Oz story and goes on to break box office records.

1959: Musical pair Richard Rodgers and Oscar Hammerstein debut *The Sound of Music.*

40   1950   1960   1970   1980   1990   2000   2010   TODAY

1937: Disney releases the first full-length animated movie—*Snow White and the Seven Dwarfs.*

1939: *Gone with the Wind*, about the Civil War, comes out. It later becomes one of the most watched films of all time.

1977: George Lucas's *Star Wars* thrills with sci-fi adventure.

2009: *Avatar* breaks ground with new filming technology.

1995: *Toy Story* is the first full-length movie created completely through computer animation.

1960s: Merce Cunningham expands abstract dance, which doesn't tell obvious stories or express feelings—that's left up to the viewer.

1970s: Alvin Ailey composes dance that draws on African American music and traditions.

2010s: Shen Wei's work surprises with moves from Chinese acrobats and martial arts.

PLAY BALL!

How big are sports in America? Big enough to bring in $440 billion a year! Let's take a closer look at how Americans enjoy their favorite pastime.

WATCH THE BIG GAME!

How many people tune in to the most watched sporting events on TV each year?

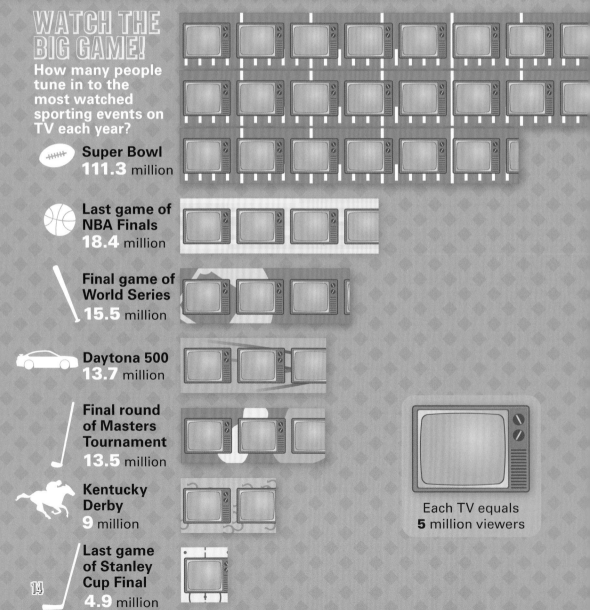

Super Bowl
111.3 million

Last game of NBA Finals
18.4 million

Final game of World Series
15.5 million

Daytona 500
13.7 million

Final round of Masters Tournament
13.5 million

Kentucky Derby
9 million

Last game of Stanley Cup Final
4.9 million

Each TV equals **5 million viewers**

KA-CHING!

Most sports stars get huge salaries. But they also cash in by promoting products, such as Nike sneakers. Here are the five US athletes who raked in the most in one recent year.

Tiger Woods

$78.1 million

Kobe Bryant

$61.9 million

LeBron James

$59.8 million

Drew Brees

$51 million

Aaron Rodgers

$49 million

GO KIDS!

About 69 percent of US girls and 75 percent of boys between the ages of eight and 17 play a team sport. What sports are most popular?

Including both boys and girls, basketball is the No. 1 kid sport in the United States.

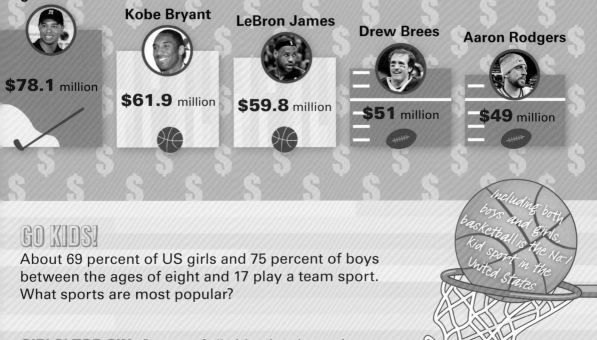

GIRLS' TOP SIX Percent of all girls who play each sport:

25	23	17	17	17	12
Basketball	Volleyball	Baseball	Soccer	Track	Swimming

BOYS' TOP SIX Percent of all boys who play each sport:

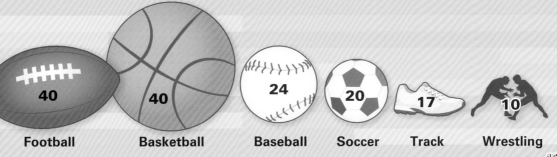

40	40	24	20	17	10
Football	Basketball	Baseball	Soccer	Track	Wrestling

WHAT TO READ?

Looking for something new to read? American authors have written some of the most-loved children's books of all time. Let this handy chart help you decide what to pick up next.

1800s

World War II → **Number the Sta** by Lois Lowry

→ **Crispin: The Cross of Lead** by Avi

survival story → **Hatchet** by Gary Paulsen

CHAPTER BOOK

back in time

about growing up

page-turners

sad

unlikely animal heroes

strange and amazing journeys

POETRY

classic funny → **Where the Sidewalk Ends** by Shel Silverstein

newer funny → **It's Raining Pigs and Noodles** by Jack Prelutsky

PICTURE BOOK

from when you were little

totally sweet

plain silly

shout it out!

friendly monsters

talking animals

Little House books
by Laura Ingalls Wilder

white point of view →

The Birchbark House
by Louise Erdrich

American Indian point of view →

serious → **Are You There God? It's Me, Margaret**
by Judy Blume

funny → **Diary of a Wimpy Kid**
by Jeff Kinney

A Series of Unfortunate Events
by Lemony Snicket

(not really) →

a little of both → **Ramona books**
by Beverly Cleary

Charlotte's Web
by E. B. White

Because of Winn-Dixie
by Kate DiCamillo

you might cry →

deep messages → **The Phantom Tollbooth**
by Norton Juster

A Wrinkle in Time
by Madeleine L'Engle

cricket →

The Cricket in Times Square
by George Selden

gorilla →

The One and Only Ivan
by Katherine Applegate

freaky flying monkeys → **The Wizard of Oz**
by L. Frank Baum

fuzzy → **Pat the Bunny**
by Dorothy Kunhardt

sleepy → **Goodnight Moon**
by Margaret Wise Brown

kind of sad too →

The Giving Tree
by Shel Silverstein

knew by heart → **Brown Bear, Brown Bear, What Do You See?**
by Bill Martin Jr.

sweetest bull ever →

The Story of Ferdinand
by Munro Leaf

adorable stuffed bear →

Corduroy
by Don Freeman

Where the Wild Things Are
by Maurice Sendak

word play →

Amelia Bedelia
by Peggy Parish

pigs → **Olivia**
by Ian Falconer

rhyme-tastic →

Green Eggs and Ham
by Dr. Seuss

Don't Let the Pigeon Drive the Bus!
by Mo Willems

llamas → **Llama Llama Red Pajama**
by Anna Dewdney

alphabet →

Chicka Chicka Boom Boom
by Bill Martin Jr. and John Archambault

amphibians → **Frog and Toad Are Friends**
by Arnold Lobel

17

LET'S CELEBRATE!

Most American holidays celebrate people—from presidents to soldiers to workers. Congress has named 10 federal holidays. School's out for most of these. Other holidays are fun to celebrate during school.

COMMON WAYS TO CELEBRATE

- Big meal
- Parties
- Fireworks
- Cookout
- Presents
- Parades
- No school in most places

- FEDERAL HOLIDAY
- JUST FOR FUN

NEW YEAR'S DAY

When: **January 1**

Fun fact: About half of America make New Year's resolutions. Losi weight is the No. 1 goal.

BIRTHDAY OF MARTIN LUTHER KING JR

When: **Third Monday in January**

Fun fact: Six million people signed a petition to make King's birthday a holiday.

APRIL

MEMORIAL DAY

When: **Last Monday in May**

Fun fact: This used to be called Decoration Day, because people decorated soldiers' graves on this day.

EARTH DAY

When: **April 22**

Fun fact: Many people go "car free" for the day.

JULY

COLUMBUS DAY

When: **Second Monday in October**

Fun fact: Several states celebrate Native American Day, or Indigenous Peoples Day, instead.

OCTOBER

HALLOWEEN

When: **October 31**

Fun fact: Candy corn is the No. 1 Halloween treat

FEBRUARY

MARCH

MAY

JUNE

AUGUST

SEPTEMBER

NOVEMBER

DECEMBER

VALENTINE'S DAY
When: **February 14**

Fun fact: Americans send about 151 million Valentine's cards every year.

ST. PATRICK'S DAY
When: **March 17**

Fun fact: As many as 250,000 people march in New York City's St. Patrick's Day parade.

WASHINGTON'S BIRTHDAY, AKA PRESIDENT'S DAY
When: **Third Monday in February**

Fun fact: This never falls on Washington's actual birthday, February 22.

LABOR DAY
When: **First Monday in September**

Fun fact: This holiday grew out of workers' fights for better pay and working conditions in the late 1800s.

INDEPENDENCE DAY
When: **July 4**

Fun fact: In the early 1800s, people celebrated with greenery instead of flags.

VETERANS DAY
When: **November 11**

Fun fact: November 11 marks the date World War I ended in 1918.

CHRISTMAS
When: **December 25**

Fun fact: The average American spends about $700 on Christmas gifts.

THANKSGIVING
When: **Last Thursday in November**

Fun fact: About 88 percent of Americans eat turkey on Thanksgiving.

19

AMERICAN LANDMARKS

Imagine the ultimate All-American road trip. What sites would be must-sees? Some places just seem to stand for what the United States is all about.

MOUNT RUSHMORE

Where: Keystone, South Dakota
Date: Completed in 1941
Stands for: The birth and growth of the United States
What to do: Come at sundown for the lighting ceremony.

Fun fact:
Each nose is about 20 feet (6 meters) high—about as tall as a two-story building.

GOLDEN GATE BRIDGE

Where: San Francisco, California
Date: 1937
Stands for: The skill and elegance of American architecture
What to do: Take in breathtaking views of San Francisco Bay.

Fun fact:
The bridge's famous orange color was chosen so it could be seen in thick fog.

Fun fact:
The amount of concrete in the dam could pave a road from San Francisco to New York.

HOOVER DAM

Where: On the Colorado River, between Arizona and Nevada
Date: 1935
Stands for: The power of American engineering
What to do: Take a tour and learn how the dam generates electricity for 1.3 million people.

STATUE OF LIBERTY

Where: Liberty Island, New York
Date: This gift from France was dedicated in 1886.
Stands for: Freedom and democracy, especially for immigrants
What to do: Climb the 354 steps to her crown.

Fun fact:
It was originally brown, like a penny. Over 30 years, the metal turned green from oxygen in the air.

SHENANDOAH

The White House
JUL 14
Washington, DC

Fun fact:
The White House is the only private home of a national leader that is open to the public.

WHITE HOUSE

Where: Washington, DC
Date: John and Abigail Adams were the first to live there, in 1800. It was rebuilt in 1817 after a fire.
Stands for: The strength and dignity of the presidential office
What to do: Take a tour—but plan ahead. Get free tickets through your US representative's office.

GREAT SMOKY MTNS.

The Lincoln Memorial
JUL 14
Washington, DC

LINCOLN MEMORIAL

Where: Washington, DC
Date: Completed in 1922
Stands for: Lincoln's legacy of unity, strength, and wisdom
What to do: Make sure to view the site from a distance. You'll see the monument and its mirror image in the Reflecting Pool.

Fun fact:
The 36 columns around the monument stand for the 36 states that were reunited after the Civil War.

National Park
JG 14

21

KNOW YOUR SYMBOLS

No doubt you could pick out the American flag in seconds. And that eagle with the ribbon in its mouth looks familiar too. But did you know that every detail of our flag and Great Seal has a special meaning? These symbols reflect the values and ideas that shaped our country.

FLAG The first official US flag was finished in 1777. The flag has changed many times as new states joined the Union. Today's flag took shape on July 4, 1960, after Hawaii became the 50th state.

Blue is for strength and justice.

There are 50 stars for 50 states.

13 stripes stand for the original 13 colonies.

White is for purity and innocence.

Red is for courage.

FLAGS ACROSS THE AGES

Until 1912, there weren't any rules about how the stars should look. That made for some creative designs.

1777	1818	1865	1912

THE GREAT SEAL

The Great Seal was designed by the Founding Fathers. They wanted a symbol to represent the young nation's ideals. The Great Seal is stamped onto treaties and other important documents that deal with foreign countries.

A new country takes its place among the "constellation" of nations.

E pluribus unum means "One out of many," in Latin. One nation formed from many states.

Front: The front side shows the nation's coat of arms. This is seen on the one-dollar bill, coins, stamps, military uniforms, passports, and monuments.

The top represents the national government.

The American bald eagle and shield represent self-reliance.

The 13 stripes stand for the first 13 states.

The olive branch and 13 arrows show the power of peace and war.

Back: This side is generally seen only on the back of the one-dollar bill.

The Eye of Providence symbolizes God watching over the Union.

Annuit coeptis means "He (God) has approved our beginnings."

The pyramid with 13 steps stands for the strength of the Union.

Roman numerals for 1776 stand for the year the Declaration of Independence was signed.

Novus ordo seclorum means "A new order of the ages."

PATRIOTIC DOS AND DON'TS

The Federal Flag Code lays out rules for how to treat our national flag, say the Pledge of Allegiance, and sing "The Star-Spangled Banner." Don't worry—you can't get arrested for doing it wrong. But it's good to know how to be a respectful citizen, so check out these pointers!

LET YOUR FLAG WAVE

DO let it wave every day, especially on the Fourth of July.

DO put it out at sunrise and take it down at sunset, or shine a light on it at night.

DON'T fly it upside down—that's like an SOS signal!

DON'T accidentally fly it halfway up the pole—that's a sign someone important has died.

RESPECT THE FLAG

DO wash it when it gets dirty.

DON'T let it touch anything beneath it—that includes countertops and piles of laundry.

DO fold it neatly and store in a clean place.

DO burn it when it is too tattered to use.

DON'T wear it or decorate it.

SALUTE THE FLAG

DO salute the flag when it passes in a parade, when it is raised or lowered, during the Pledge of Allegiance, and during the national anthem.

DO stand up and put your right hand over your heart.

DON'T worry about saluting if your arm's in a cast or you're holding a baby—just do your best!

DON'T do a military hand salute unless you are a soldier or a veteran.

SAY THE PLEDGE OF ALLEGIANCE

DO take off your hat, salute the flag, and say the words loud and proud.

DON'T be THAT loud— you don't want to drown out others' voices!

SING OUR NATIONAL ANTHEM

DO face the flag, not the singer (unless there's no flag).

DON'T be afraid to sing along, even on those high notes!

PROTECT MY RIGHTS!

"It's a free country!" Have you ever yelled that at someone? Well, it's true. American citizens (especially adults) get to say, wear, go, and do what they want—mostly. Their actions still can't harm their neighbors. As Americans, we have specific rights. What are these rights, exactly? The First Amendment of the Bill of Rights spells out five basic freedoms. Check out how these rights play out in everyday life.

KEY

 ? Up for debate

 STOP How freedom is limited

 Court says

 Makes you wonder

People have the right to say what they want.

 SPEECH

STOP Speech that creates a "clear and present danger" is not allowed. You can't yell "Fire!" in a crowded movie theater when there isn't a fire.

STOP Teachers can still punish students for what they say (or for talking too much).

? Words or actions that are extremely offensive are called hate speech. They may include using racist words (in speech, graffiti, etc.) against someone. Should they ever be illegal? In what situations?

In general, people have the right to criticize, insult, and make fun of one another.

People can ask the government to fix a problem or right a wrong.

Have you ever signed a petition? Or sent a message to a member of Congress? It's your basic right!

People have the right to join private groups.

STOP **The group can't attack people or do other violent things.**

STOP **Groups can't be disruptive. For example, you can't block traffic or trample someone's lawn.**

Even groups based on racist ideas are allowed to meet.

During the civil rights movement, police in South Carolina arrested a group of African American protesters at the state capitol. The police argued the group might cause a riot. In 1963, the Supreme Court ruled the police had violated the peaceful group's right to assembly.

PETITION

ASSEMBLY

FIVE BASIC FREEDOMS

PRESS

RELIGION

Reporters, authors, and artists are free to express themselves. The government does not run the media.

STOP **Newspapers can't tell lies on purpose.**

? **Is it okay for newspapers to print government secrets? Who decides what's a secret?**

In 1988, the Supreme Court ruled that a principal in Missouri could ban topics in a school newspaper.

The government stays out of how you practice a religion. It doesn't force any religion on you.

? **Is it okay for students to pray at school? If so, when and how?**

In 2000, the Supreme Court ruled that students in Texas couldn't lead prayers over the school's loudspeaker.

BE A STAR CITIZEN

As a US citizen, your basic freedoms are protected. So what can you give back to your country? Being a good citizen means caring for the people and places around you. It also means learning about our country and speaking up when things are wrong. Here are some ways kids can give a little or a lot:

Clean up your garbage.

Call 911 if you see someone in an emergency.

BASIC DUTIES

IT'S THE LAW

Learn all the states and their capitals.

Recycle cans and bottles.

Wait for a walk signal before crossing the street.

Show up at school ready to learn and **do your best**.

Donate cans or other nonperishable food to a food drive.

Visit a neighbor who might be lonely.

Read a book to someone who can't.

Write a letter to your state or US representative. Tell your representative your opinion on an issue you care about.

Host a party for all the little kids in your neighborhood.

HERO

EXTRA MILE

Start a **food drive** at your school.

Speak up when you see someone being bullied.

Make a **thank-you gift** for your teacher.

Go with your parents when they **vote**.

Read the Bill of Rights with an adult.

Join a **cleanup crew** at a local park.

ARE YOU UP TO THE TEST?

Each year, about 700,000 immigrants become US citizens. Most of them have to pass a test about US facts and history. Here are some real questions from the test. How did you do?

1. What is an amendment?
2. What are the two parts of the US Congress?
3. In what month do we vote for president?
4. What group of people was taken to America and sold as slaves?
5. Who was the first president?
6. What ocean is on the East Coast of the United States?
7. When do we celebrate Independence Day?
8. Why does the flag have 50 stars?

THE ANSWERS TO THE QUIZ ARE ON PAGE 32.

 Glossary

AMENDMENT: a change to the US Constitution. The First Amendment protects free speech and other forms of expression.

ANTHEM: a song of praise. A national anthem is also a key symbol of a country.

BILL OF RIGHTS: the first ten amendments to the US Constitution. The Bill of Rights protects individual freedoms, such as free speech.

BROADWAY: an area in New York City, around a street called Broadway, where many of the world's most famous musicals are performed

FOOD DRIVE: a charity effort where people come together and donate food items to those in need

IMMIGRANT: a person who came from one country to live in a new one. The United States has been a haven for immigrants.

JAZZ: a form of music developed by African Americans. Many jazz artists perform music they make up on the spot.

MINORITY: a group of people of a certain race, religion, or ethnic group living among a larger group of a different race, religion, or ethnic group

MUSICAL: a form of theater that tells a story through both talking and singing

PETITION: to request a change in policy. A petition can also be a document, signed by many, that lays out such a request.

REPRESENTATIVE: an elected lawmaker. A representative serves the voters from his or her home district.

RODEO: an event where people compete at riding horses and bulls, roping calves, and performing other shows of skillful animal handling

SALUTE: to honor someone or something with a hand motion or other gesture

SCAT: to sing nonsense sounds instead of words. Louis Armstrong was a master at scatting.

SELF-RELIANCE: trust in one's own efforts and abilities

VETERAN: a person who has fought in a war

Cahill, Bryon. *Freedom of Speech and Expression.* South Egremont, MA: Red Chair Press, 2013. Learn more about one of the most prized freedoms in US culture.

Encyclopedia Smithsonian: Kid Favorites
http://www.si.edu/Encyclopedia/Search/Kids%20Favorites
This site is a grab bag of fun information and activities about US culture. Tour the American Art Museum, design a Puerto Rican carnival mask, read about famous horses, and more.

Higgins, Nadia. *US Geography through Infographics.* Minneapolis: Lerner Publications, 2015. Dig into more fact-packed infographics, and learn how where we live shapes our lives and culture.

Internet Movie Database: Musicals
http://www.imdb.com/genre/musical
This site combines two all-American art forms: movies and musicals. Scroll through a list of favorite musicals on film. Watch trailers, read reviews, and more.

McHugh, Erin. *National Parks: A Kid's Guide to America's Parks, Monuments, and Landmarks.* New York: Black Dog & Leventhal Publishers, 2012. Check out this fun, fact-packed guide to more than 75 sites every kid wants to see.

Orgill, Roxane. *Skit-Scat Raggedy Cat: Ella Fitzgerald.* Somerville, MA: Candlewick Press, 2010. Read the amazing story of this American jazz legend.

Sports Illustrated Kids
http://www.sikids.com
Watch videos, play games, enter contests, and get the latest news on your favorite sports teams.

Symbols of US Government
http://bensguide.gpo.gov/3-5/symbols
This official site for kids is a great first stop for report research. Find quick, reliable facts on patriotic songs, symbols, statues, and key government buildings.

Walker, Paul Robert. *A Nation of Immigrants.* New York: Kingfisher, 2012. Learn the story of how the United States became the most diverse nation in the world.

White House Virtual Tour
http://www.whitehouse.gov/about/inside-white-house/interactive-tour
It's the same tour as the real-life one, only you get to click on what you want to see instead of walking around.

Index

American flag, 22, 24–25

Bill of Rights, 26–27
books and reading, 16–17

cities and towns, 7, 8–9
citizenship and duties, 28–29

dance, 9, 12–13

ethnic groups, 6, 8–9

freedom. *See* Bill of Rights
free time. *See* relaxation

Golden Gate Bridge, 20
Great Seal, 23

Halloween, 18
holidays, 18–19

Independence Day, 18–19

landmarks, 20–21
languages, 6

Mount Rushmore, 20
movies, 12–13
music, 12–13

National Anthem, 25

pets, 7
Pledge of Allegiance, 25

relaxation, 10–11
religion, 6, 27

sports, 14–15
Statue of Liberty, 21
symbols, 22–23

television, 10–11, 14–15
Thanksgiving, 19
theater, 12–13
types of families, 7

Valentine's Day, 19

PHOTO ACKNOWLEDGMENTS
The images in this book are used with the permission of: © Pete Niesen /Shutterstock.com, p. 8 (top); © Mariusz Jurgielewicz/Dreamstime.com, p. 8 (middle); Korean Culture and Information Service/Wikimedia Commons, p. 8 (bottom); JEFF KOWALSKY/EPA/Newscom, p. 9 (top); AP Photo/Michael Dwyer, p. 9 (bottom); © Dgareri/Dreamstime.com, p. 15 (LeBron James); © Sbukley /Dreamstime.com, p. 15 (Tiger Woods, Kobe Bryant); © Mat Hayward /Shutterstock.com, p. 15 (Aaron Rodgers); © Wesley Hitt/Getty Images Sport /Getty Images, p. 15 (Drew Brees); National Archives pp. 26–27 (background).

ANSWERS TO QUIZ ON PAGE 29: 1) a change to the US Constitution, 2) the Senate and the US House of Representatives, 3) November, 4) Africans, 5) George Washington, 6) Atlantic Ocean, 7) July 4, 8) for 50 states